BOUBLIL AND SCHÖNBERG's Lege

Les Misérables™

THE MUSICAL THAT SWEPT THE WORLD
— IN CONCERT —

CAMERON MACKINTOSH Presents
A Musical by
ALAIN BOUBLIL & CLAUDE-MICHEL SCHÖNBERG

based on the novel by VICTOR HUGO

Music by CLAUDE-MICHEL SCHÖNBERG
Original French Lyrics by ALAIN BOUBLIL
and JEAN-MARC NATEL
English Lyrics by HERBERT KRETZMER

Additional material by JAMES FENTON
Orchestral score by JOHN CAMERON

Designed by JOHN NAPIER
Lighting by DAVID HERSEY
Costumes by ANDREANE NEOFITOU

Directed and Adapted by
TREVOR NUNN & JOHN CAIRD

THE MUSICAL SENSATION
1987 "TONY" AWARD BEST MUSICAL

ISBN 978-0-634-05003-9

ALAIN BOUBLIL MUSIC LTD.
c/o Joel Faden and Company Inc., 1775 Broadway, New York, NY 10019

EXCLUSIVELY DISTRIBUTED BY

HAL•LEONARD®
CORPORATION
7777 W. BLUEMOUND RD. P.O. BOX 13819 MILWAUKEE, WI 53213

Dramatic Performance Rights controlled and licensed by Cameron Mackintosh (Overseas) Ltd.,
One Bedford Square, London WC1B 3RA England
Tel (171) 637-8866 Fax (171) 436-2683

Stock and Amateur Performance Rights are licensed by
Music Theater International, Inc.
545 Eighth Avenue, New York, New York 10018
Tel (212) 868-6668 Fax (212) 643-8465

Non-Dramatic and Concert Performance Rights are controlled
by Alain Boublil Music Ltd. and licensed by the American
Society of Composers, Authors and Publishers (ASCAP),
One Lincoln Plaza, New York, New York 10023
Tel (212) 595-3050 Fax (212) 787-1381

CONTENTS

What Have I Done?

Music by CLAUDE-MICHEL SCHÖNBERG
Lyrics by ALAIN BOUBLIL, JEAN-MARC NATEL and HERBERT KRETZMER

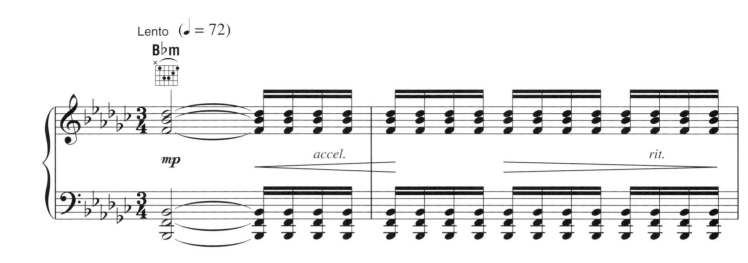

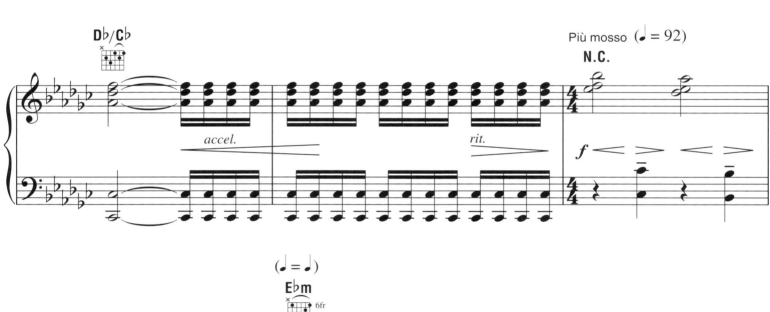

VALJEAN:

What have I done,_ sweet Je-sus, what have I done?_ Be-come a

known.

Tempo primo

One word from him and I'd be back beneath the lash, upon the

rack, Instead he offers me my freedom. I

feel my shame in-side me like a knife.___ He told me that I have a

soul, how does he know?

What spir-it comes to move my life, is there an-oth-er way to

Lento - recitative

go? I am reach-ing but I fall and the night is clos-ing in and I

At the End of the Day

Music by CLAUDE-MICHEL SCHÖNBERG
Lyrics by ALAIN BOUBLIL, JEAN-MARC NATEL and HERBERT KRETZMER

I Dreamed a Dream

Music by CLAUDE-MICHEL SCHÖNBERG
Lyrics by ALAIN BOUBLIL, JEAN-MARC NATEL and HERBERT KRETZMER

Lovely Ladies

Music by CLAUDE-MICHEL SCHÖNBERG
Lyrics by ALAIN BOUBLIL, JEAN-MARC NATEL and HERBERT KRETZMER

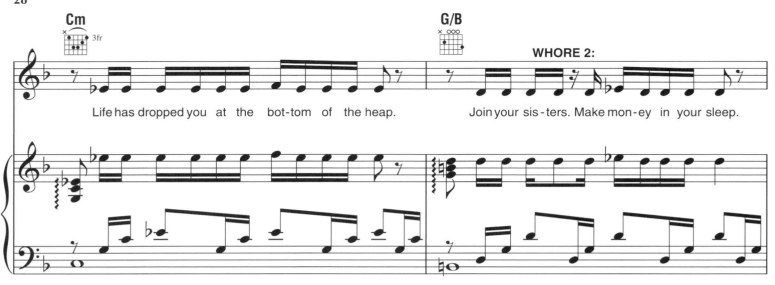

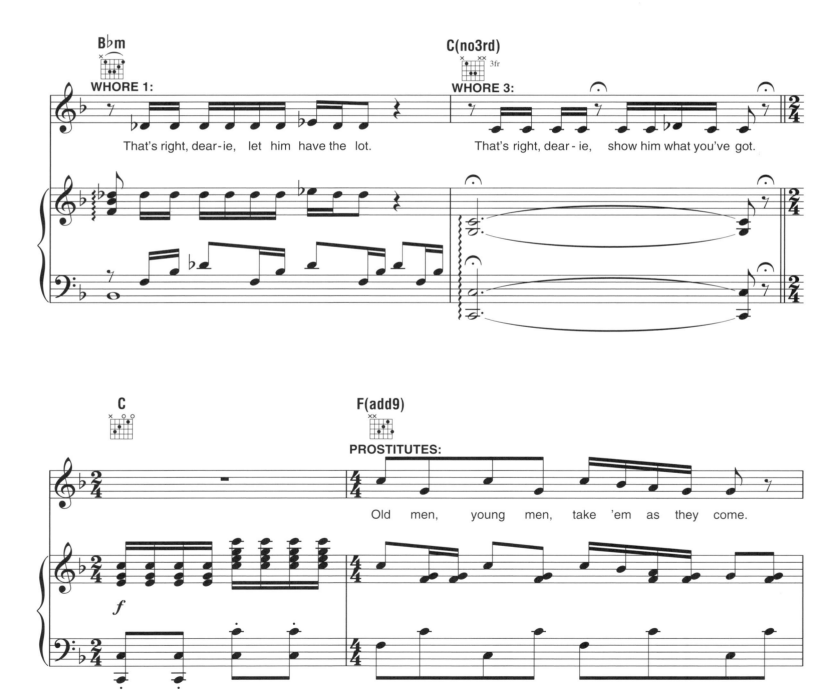

Don't it make a change to have a girl who can't re-fuse? Eas-y mon-ey,

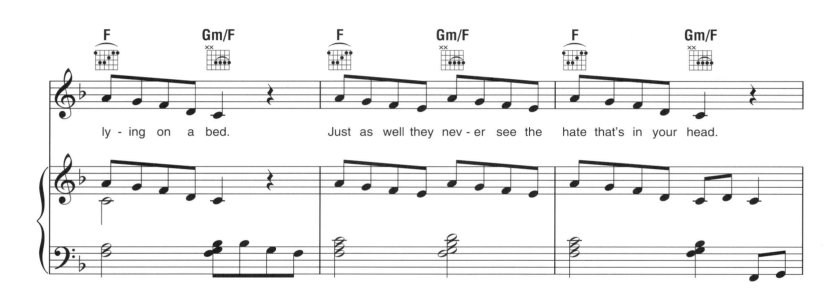

ly-ing on a bed. Just as well they nev-er see the hate that's in your head.

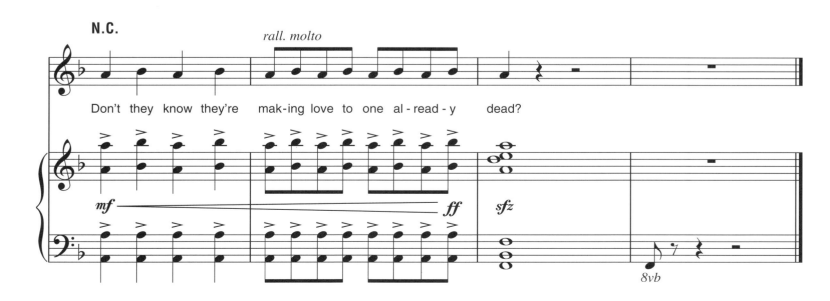

Don't they know they're mak-ing love to one al-read-y dead?

Come to Me
(Fantine's Death)

Music by CLAUDE-MICHEL SCHÖNBERG
Lyrics by ALAIN BOUBLIL, JEAN-MARC NATEL and HERBERT KRETZMER

Lento

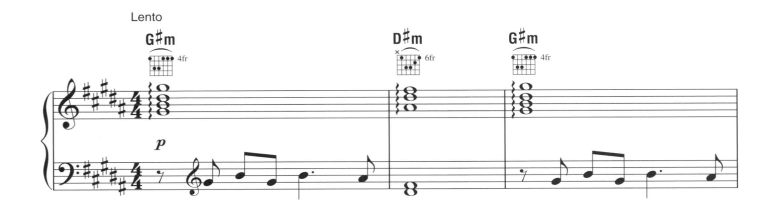

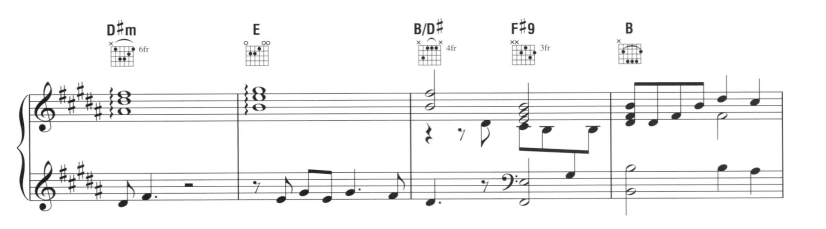

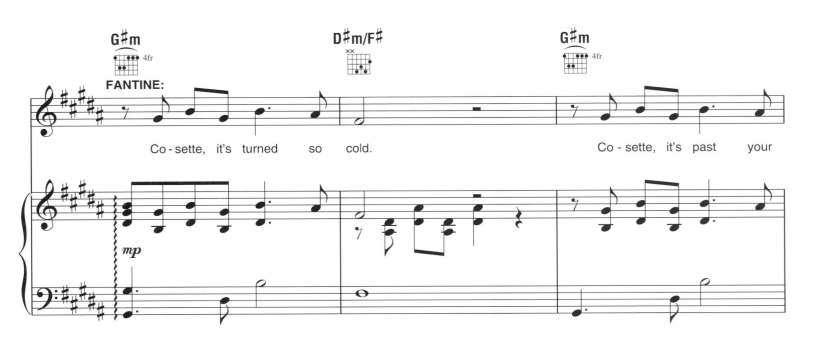

FANTINE:

Co - sette, it's turned so cold.   Co - sette, it's past your

Castle on a Cloud

Music by CLAUDE-MICHEL SCHÖNBERG
Lyrics by ALAIN BOUBLIL, JEAN-MARC NATEL and HERBERT KRETZMER

COSETTE:

There is a cas - tle on a cloud.
There is a room that's full of toys.

I like to go there in my sleep.
There are a hun - dred boys and girls.

The Thénardier Waltz of Treachery

Music by CLAUDE-MICHEL SCHÖNBERG
Lyrics by ALAIN BOUBLIL, JEAN-MARC NATEL and HERBERT KRETZMER

sette.   It   won't   take   you   too   long   to   for - get.

f a tempo

rall.

47

there's a cas - tle just wait - ing for you.

Look Down

Music by CLAUDE-MICHEL SCHÖNBERG
Lyrics by ALAIN BOUBLIL, JEAN-MARC NATEL and HERBERT KRETZMER

PIMP: Leave the poor old cow, move it, Mad - e - leine, she used to be no bet - ter till the

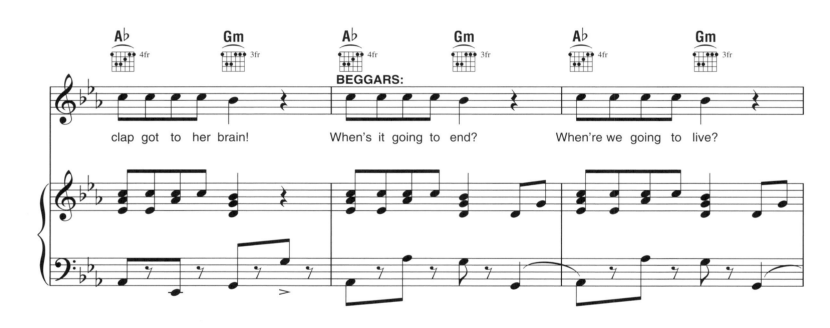

clap got to her brain! BEGGARS: When's it going to end? When're we going to live?

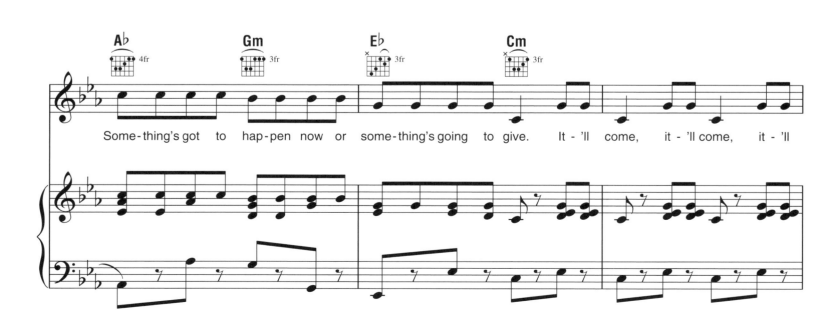

Some-thing's got to hap-pen now or some-thing's going to give. It - 'll come, it - 'll come, it - 'll

54

56

Red and Black

Music by CLAUDE-MICHEL SCHÖNBERG
Lyrics by ALAIN BOUBLIL, JEAN-MARC NATEL and HERBERT KRETZMER

ENJOLRAS:
It is time for us all to de-cide who we are.

Do we fight for the right to a night at the op-er-a now?

Have you asked of your-selves what's the price you might pay?

Do You Hear the People Sing?

Music by CLAUDE-MICHEL SCHÖNBERG
Lyrics by ALAIN BOUBLIL, JEAN-MARC NATEL and HERBERT KRETZMER

On My Own

Music by CLAUDE-MICHEL SCHÖNBERG
Lyrics by ALAIN BOUBLIL, JOHN CAIRD,
TREVOR NUNN, JEAN-MARC NATEL and HERBERT KRETZMER

68

A Heart Full of Love

Music by CLAUDE-MICHEL SCHÖNBERG
Lyrics by ALAIN BOUBLIL, JEAN-MARC NATEL and HERBERT KRETZMER

One Day More

Music by CLAUDE-MICHEL SCHÖNBERG
Lyrics by ALAIN BOUBLIL, JEAN-MARC NATEL and HERBERT KRETZMER

Bring Him Home

Music by CLAUDE-MICHEL SCHÖNBERG
Lyrics by ALAIN BOUBLIL and HERBERT KRETZMER

Empty Chairs at Empty Tables

Music by CLAUDE-MICHEL SCHÖNBERG
Lyrics by ALAIN BOUBLIL and HERBERT KRETZMER

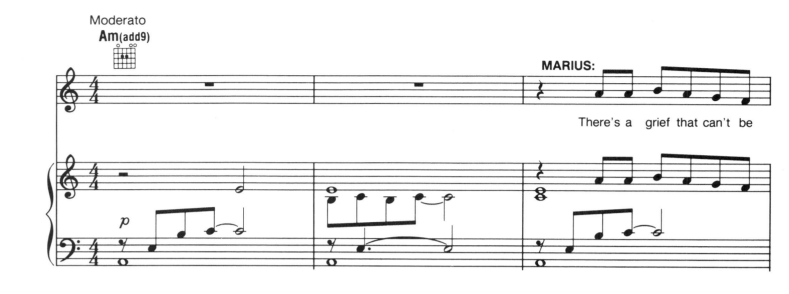

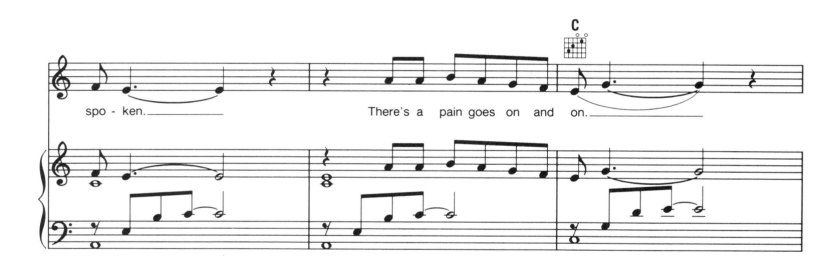

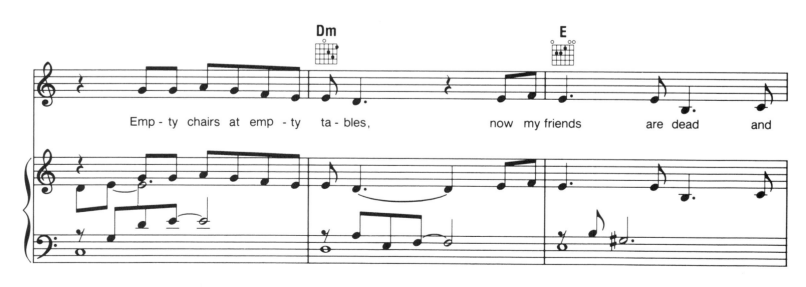

Little People

Music by CLAUDE-MICHEL SCHÖNBERG
Lyrics by ALAIN BOUBLIL, JEAN-MARC NATEL and HERBERT KRETZMER

They

laugh at me, these fel - lows, Just be - cause I am small. _____ They
li - ath was a bruis - er who was tall as the sky _____ but

laugh at me be - cause I'm not a hun - dred feet tall! _____ I
Da - vid threw a right and gave him one in the eye. _____ I